intermodulations

poems by

Steve Carter

Copyright © 2014 Steve Carter

All rights reserved.

ISBN 978-0-9960302-2-9

Maat Publishing
1 Crown Point Drive
Dover, NH 03820
contact@maatpublishing.net
www.maatpublishing.net

Contents

act one   1
each is both   2
prana   3
standing room   4
Betsy   5
"Room in Brooklynn, 1932"   6
composition   8
Syncretistic Poem   9
reflex   10
Rooms   11
Meditation in Black   12
Dreamvoyage to the Isle of the Dead   13
attempt at dialogue   14
construction sight   15
a voice crying in the wilderness   16
A Day Out   17
Ceremony #1   18
portrait   19
curiosity   20
The Persistence of Memory   21
Lump/Son of Lump   22
Depth Perception   23
Working in Boston   24
The Singer   26
Warmup   27
while you were gone   28
another poem written in the laundromat   29
How was your day?   30
Inexpressible Joy   31
A Poem in the Making   32
bedrock tidalwave   33
Dancing under the Stars   35
Fishing in Florida   36
Love Song   37

reflections 38
wiping the leaves 40
The Gift 41
Song in Two Movements 46
Southern Florida in Two Dimensions 49
Serenade 50
Remembrance 51

Acknowledgements

Thanks to Jo-el Gavel (happymessyes@gmail.com) for the cover artwork. Thanks to Wendy Carter for the blurb on the back of the book. And my deepest gratitude and love to my wife, Marilynn, and our two daughters, Sheri and Wendy, for inspiring so many of these poems, and for supporting all my artistic pursuits.

Thanks also to the editors of the following journals in which some of these poems were first published:

Artzone	*composition*
Artzone	*Dreamvoyage to the Isle of the Dead*
Carolina Quarterly	*Syncretistic Poem*
Chiron Review	*A Voice Crying in the Wilderness*
Clackamas Literary Review	*Warmup*
Clackamas Literary Review	*reflections*
Dark Horse	*Standing Room*
Earthwise: A Journal of Poetry	*Room in Brooklyn 1932*
Hanging Loose	*Merry Go Round*
Hiram Poetry Review	*reflex*
LSR	*curiosity*
Mobius	*construction sight*
Montage	*Dear Mr President*
New Magazine	*Betsy*
Orphic Lute	*wiping the leaves*
Pacific Review	*portrait*
Stand Magazine	*Rooms*
The Cortland Review	*The Singer*
The New Renaissance	*A Day Out*
Wind	*prana*
Wisconsin Review	*Attempt at Dialog*
Wisconsin Review	*bedrock tidalwave*

Act One

"not to act for fear of failure - that is the greatest mistake"

  today the air stings
  as it should
  this time of year
  I was glad of the chance
  the chore of getting
  the Sunday paper
    (all the time watching myself
    my words)
  limited by my technique
  yet it is just that
  that precipitates
  awareness
  to care only
  about awareness
  or if possible
  not even that
  yes not even that
  but only that
  something
  is better
  than to want and
  not

  who is it for?

  itself
  and no other
    (the silence in the temple room
    the chapel organ music
    solitude

    the ability to be alone

        an art dearly come by

each is both

the music of poetry
the poetry of music

the one who sings
and the one who listens

Prana

    1.

10:25 A.M., bus stop

fingers to lips slightly parted
inhale   the cool air
the woman in front of me
fingering her rosary beads   lips parting   slightly
asking questions compulsively   scowling
the answers are never quite enough
her mind racing   to quiet her mind
"(Hail Mary)...has the Chestnut Hill bus...
(full of grace)...gone by...(the Lord is
with thee)...yet?"

    2.

10:25 P.M., Cable Car (night club)

the student of religion at the front table
pipe between lips slightly parted
tobacco flavored with whiskey
listening to the music

listening

listening

Standing Room

this bus is crowded
always

my excuse for sitting
is reading
this book

eyes cast down
so as
not to see

faces
scowling
down

Betsy

so
i was just sitting there
on the grass not
knowing anyone when this girl
sat down beside me
and said something
like

> hi my name is betsy today is the first day i have been happy
> since the boy who gave me this bell i like this bell it's like
> me noisy and open and meaningful or less depending on where
> you are went into the attic to meditate his mind never came
> down from the attic are you happy being yourself i wonder if
> i could catch the sun in this bell they say the sun is very
> big it only looks as big as the end of my finger which this
> bell is bigger than if i was going to write a song i would say
> happiness is the best smog control

                                              and

then her friends called her
and she said
goodbye and kissed me on the
cheek and left and i
thought oh well i
don't have to worry
if the sun ever falls
old betsy will catch it

in her bell.

"Room in Brooklynn, 1932"
Edward Hopper (American) 1882-1967

Three windows.
Three shades,
drawn to different levels,
different shades
of green.

Blue sky
cut
by window frames.
The flat roofs (chimneys, short dark chimneys)
buildings across, dark brick,
windows dark.

The three windows form a corner
of the room.
The woman sits, her back to us,
in her rocking chair,
still, on the left.
In the corner,
framed by the windows,
a vase of flowers
on a three-legged table
with a hanging green cloth
sits.
The vase white,
flowers pink
embedded in greens.
Blue dress. Dark
closer to us, left,
a flat table, crimson cloth,
rounding over corners,
hangs.

Through the window
 on the right
 falling on the carpet
 in a perfect rectangle
 (except for the shadow,
 a dark ellipse,
 of the still dark dress)
 touching the sill
 gold as it passes,
 turning bright
 green as it falls on the carpet:
                    light

composition

a light bulb   hangs   under
its shade   from the ceiling
the shadow cast   above   on the ceiling
ceiling   below   beneath
the chair   the shade is blue
the chair yellow   both shadows
are grey

Syncretistic Poem

i would paint
        like a child

a flat table
        with no legs

craft   crafted   craft   crafty

I will paint the table brown,
   the legs can stay the color they are.

reflex

The greatest poverty is not to live
In a physical world.
　　　　　-Wallace Stevens

    one man
    studying
    two pears

    is two pears
    studying one man

    each

Rooms

Rooms
open
onto each other.

In some
footsteps echo.

Dust collects itself
and its echoes.

Dim light passes
from room to room
with infinite
patience.

The opening
of a door
forms
walls, floor, ceiling

and the next door,
always closed,
waiting

or perhaps
just closing,
shutting out
the light.

Meditation in Black

The young priest
alone on the sidewalk
clean black
white square of collar
shining black hair combed straight
eyes not lifted
face grim, straight ahead
walks swiftly, alone.

I, too, want to fall back
on someone else's words
(where was it I read that story of the priests
who knew it was all a lie? In the same book
with "The Land of the Blind." Thinking
of one-eyed Christ, the king.) No-
I can't use that, can't
allow myself
such luxury.
  Rather say-
    my friend, the "witness", talking
    of Anti-Christ, who will be,
    the Bible says, an intellectual.
    Dangerous. Seductive.

            Weaver of the wind.

Dreamvoyage to the Isle of the Dead

"Crossing is never easy," he was saying.
"The space between the shores frightens us all,
though it is filled with water," pulling on the oars.
I (?) remembered the perfumes and sperm,
the long lighted tunnel, voices, those gone before, all.
The light, the insistent light, speaking...
Pulling, he spoke: "My boat is a pram; blunt at both ends;
looks the same coming and going,"
Janus spoke.

attempt at dialogue

"Why don't you
answer me
when I
talk to you?"

voice deep
from wanting
to ask more

other accumulations

some
now
past
time

dark
beyond remembering

the vibration
of each voice
speaking its own
identity

regardless
of the words

the reach of answer
conditioned
by the frame
of the question

reaching
beyond words

beyond questioning

construction sight

there are those minds
that can stand
nothing
that is open

in a sandy lot
an unfinished building
with a great hole
where the door should be
inside
bare walls
rafters

it is evening
a man stands
staring into it
shaking his head
asking,
    "Why isn't it finished?"

A Voice Crying in the Wilderness

on the corner of Mass Ave & Boylston
a tall thin black man
sways his sax to & fro
nearly hitting me as I pass
his bony chest exposed
to the wind
blowing in off the Mass Pike

he once saw a commercial
about how Sonny Rollins
stood on the Brooklyn Bridge
and practiced
night after night
blowing into the East River

until he got so good
they made a TV commercial about him

A Day Out

the same fool

on the bus

going out of our town   and

going out of their town   talking to himself

knows how to tell jokes

discuss politics

drop names

the most frightening part:

he met another fool   they understood each other

    (that is not the worst:

        they were the only ones

        not afraid to speak)

in the museum

    Van Gogh's flowers

    Renoir's dancers

    the plagues of Egypt

    Picasso's Minotaurs

Ceremony #1

Two young men,
one in shirtsleeves,
carry an old TV
out of the repair shop
face down,
the cord dragging
on the ground.

It is saturday morning.
Grey clouds have gathered

They place the TV
in a panel truck,
face down,
cover it
with a dark cloth.

portrait

in a room   where I have never been

you polish your dreams

your secrets are not my secrets

what do you really look like

when you are alone?

curiosity

polyvalent

able
to connect
at many points

potentialities
distributed throughout

open
bonding

The Persistence of Memory

a (once) Japanese soldier lost
in the jungles of the Phillipines   today
surrendered his sword
twenty-nine years after
the end of the war

the (former japanese) Soldier would
not surrender except under order
from his superior who is
(now) a Japanese book-
seller and had to be flown in.

his (the Soldier's, formerly Japanese) sword
was accepted by the man who had
fought so bitterly against the (once) Japs

he (formerly Japanese, once Soldier) had kept
a strict
military
alert
ate only bananas

when asked if there had been any enjoyable times in the jungle
he (   ) said   no   today
was the happiest day of his life.

Lump/Son of Lump

Lump

a lump on my forehead
the size of half a grape   not so purple
right next to the scar left by chickenpox, age six.
I walked around with it for days   weeks
fearing that everyone(who of course stared at me)
would stare at me   could see through it   right into my head:
all my frustrations   confusion   dirty thoughts
on display

fortunately, it was opaque
letting nothing out
but a little blood
under the surgeon's knife

Son of Lump

you returned in the night
this time to stay
settled under the shadow
of the brow
smaller now
a shadow of your former self

I guess I'll grow
to love you

Depth Perception

when he sat next to you
and spoke
his voice was always
in the next room

or, at best,
under the table
where his eyes
seemed to be looking,
over the top of his wine glass
through the table's dark wood

you could never tell
which of you
he did not want to hear

Working in Boston
(jazz recitative)

working in Boston
a musician   a daygig
working in Boston

teaching at Berklee
so many guitarists
working in Boston

walk down Boylston St.
see so many faces
trying to make places
for themselves
working in Boston

me too
another face
no other place
just Boston

tonight a rehearsal
like so many others
music from every floor
every door closed to the rest
our poster on the wall
next to so many others
all alike all alike
next to so many other
closed doors

tomorrow night a concert
like so many others
not
like so many others
for me

I will be there
play there
try not to try
too hard
like all the other
nights
all the other
concerts
all the other
tries
not for all the others
for me
this one's for me

working
in Boston

The Singer

holds down
two jobs

"to make ends meet"
he says

days
he teaches children
not
   to dance
       between the earth's dark pull
          and the bright moon's longing
but to walk
     in their appointed places

nights he entertains
chattering customers
put down their strong drinks
to stumble to the dance floor

late
when the music has faded
into darkness
he sits on the edge of his bed
listening
for the sound
of his own voice

Warmup

maybe nothing.
maybe just an exercise.

but an exercise
as a warmup for a dance
is
or can become
the dance

we feel the body move
within the air
of a room

feel the body's push
against the resistance
of the floor
feel the body
sculpt out shapes
within the space defined
by walls, ceiling, floor.

exploration, discovery
of the body
through space.

>though the exercise
>may be repeated
>"exactly as before"
>every day,
>
>the dancer hopes
>that the room
>has windows
>
>that the light may fall
>differently
>each day.

while you were gone

a knot in my chest
speaks of hunger
as yet untasted

I pick up the phone
    we talk
I put down the phone

there is a shadow
between myself
and my laughter

I cannot speak your name

I am not the prince:
with the tip of my sword
I worry the knot

another poem written in the laundromat
(for my wife)

my father hated laundromats
would always put the clothes in and
go directly across the street to the barroom
he saw no reason to go home
to a wife he couldn't please
and two sons he could not get interested in
so he sat in the barroom directly
across from the laundromat talking
loudly over the television and the jukebox
with the other men who were waiting
for their laundry to wash or dry and
not wanting to go home to their wives who they could not etc.
all of which made for a very full barroom
and a very empty laundromat

but here I sit in the laundromat
waiting for my clothes to dry not
going directly across the street to
the barroom which is of course
inevitably located directly across from
every laundromat or else where
could the men go after putting their
shirts and socks in to wash or dry except
home to their wives who they cannot etc.
but I am here in this laundromat
as opposed to that barroom all of which is
to say that if it was not raining like hell out
I would be home with you now
because unlike them and my father too
I love you

How was your day?

the problem being
survival priorities
are not the same
as necessities
for contentment

today frustration
set in early
flowing out
in ragged lines.
  make them play   my music
  that's a nice tune

first student no show
I spend his time
working it out more
Bach's flowing lines
raggedly
a chromatic approach
to the problem

un
re
solved

a cadence
into evening
with you

Inexpressible Joy

is as common
as watching my daughter
eat cantaloupe
her face dripping
with the orange
life of the fruit

a smile
behind the rind's
wide crescent

A Poem in the Making
    (for Wendy)

We named you well.
How did we know that you would touch the earth
differently,
that gravity would need to renegotiate with you
at each step?

You dance from day to surprising day,
everyone near
touched by the air
you have stirred.

You draw a white horse curving its long neck
To drink from a blue stream that flows through a country
Known only to you,
And ask, "But haven't you seen her?"
Somehow we know we have,
Or will.

In the mute runes
Of tree bark
I try to read
The journal of your days.

bedrock tidalwave

1. arteries

in a closed system
away
means
toward

your voice echoes
against the skin of memory

if I follow
far enough

2. veins

the eye sees
and imitates
a form
evolved
out of rock
touched deeply
by music

reaching
through
layer after layer
time's orchestrations

lines drawn
on the face
crowsfeet of care
erode the eyes

3. chamber music

when I sing to you
you smile

the earth cracks

ever so slightly

Dancing under the Stars

under the wide southern sky
the moon so far away
a few puffs of cloud
like the wisps of white hair
on the head of an old man

on the boardwalk
a bandstand
a trio of old players:

drummer fat, comfortable
behind his set and mic, singing
always just behind the beat

accordian player(old electric
not a Cordovox) always loosing himself
his notes lost in the maze
of outdated electronics, playing
the wrong chords he learned
twenty years ago
or more

trumpeter, the only live wire
playing too many rips, always
the same embellishments
all the old tricks
blues licks
out of place
out of time

as we walk away
our three-year-old dances
jubilantly in the sand
her older sister bends
to pick up a seashell
glistening in the moonlight

Fishing in Florida

Though the clouds are grey,
heavy with immanent rain,
though the waters of the Intercoastal
flow steadily past,
though I am alone,
it is quiet,
I have time--
yet I am dry.

This morning I flew out of Boston,
where poems are still
immanent in the late afternoon air,
while here there is only grey sky
and the threat of rain.

A man walks by in swim trunks,
beach jacket, sandles,
carrying a fishing rod
with a bright orange bobber,
and a bright orange tackle box.
He, no doubt, will catch a fish.

Love Song

Your voice floating
through my dreams this morning.
I wake to see you standing
next to the bed,
wearing my bathrobe,
much too big for you,
your smile reflecting
the warmth it gives you.

May my love always wrap around you
like that.

reflections

I bring rules
that bind me
too tight

sight strained
by too strong
a desire to see

ripples on water
form no pattern
I can see

holding no single
wave I can ride

trees
deep-rooted
having withstood hurricanes
now stand
firm
on old roots

a few trees blown down
roots horizontal
exposed, still
live
send new trunks
straight up
compete with younger trees
for the scant sunlight

birds float
on water

far from here
the vines of a banyan tree
reach
toward earth
each to become
a trunk

one
of many

roots
trunks
past, present, future
still water
seemingly
flowing deeply
to the sea

memories refusing to rise
consciousness refusing to
sink into memory

all
is emptiness

reaching

wiping the leaves

the spider plant
hangs

high on the wall
near our bed

far from the light
from the windows

it has not grown
in years

I wipe years
of dust

from its waxy
leaves

so they may
breathe

gently

afraid of breaking
what little life
they have left

though in the jungle
this plant would
stand up
under
full tropical rains

in here it collects
only dust

The Gift

1.

trying to remember my grandfather
I see only hands

a square thumb
stained yellow-brown
from stuffed pipes
calloused
from split wood
and skate blades
   tested for sharpness
   after careful filing

knotted fingers
reach into a deep pocket
pull out a small bag of change
grey with use
   once it was white
   and bore the name of a bank
   in sharp black letters

   . . .

the arrow cost a quarter

when it left the bow
its feathers cut my hand
leaving
between my thumb and finger
a fine red line

2.

black skates
silver blades gleaming in the sun

black ice stretched tight
from shore to shore

your voice calling back to me
over your shoulder
puffs of white in the stinging air
your hands folded behind your back

the blade hangs still
for a moment
as the cellist's bow
on the upstroke
prepares the next deep tone

flashes down
curving outward
cutting
in the sleek black ice
a new line of silver
not parallel to the last
yet never to meet

as the strings of the cello
widen
taut
near the bridge
to send their tone
shivering through the dark body

you taught me to point outward
always outward
to push
not to think of going ahead
but to push
and glide
hands folded behind your back

I soon learned
to follow your smooth motion
across the black frozen lake
trying always to shape my lines
like yours
a graceful curve
outward
first toward one shore
then the other

at the end of each stroke
the blade shivered the ice
with a quick push

splinters of ice
flashing in the sun

3.

"Put your thumb along one side and your fingers
along the other, but keep them folded in so they're
out of the way of the blade. That's it. Now, with
this hand hold the blade between your thumb and
finger and pull it out. When you get it halfway
out it will catch, then grip it more firmly and
pull it all the way out. OK? Go ahead."

from the strain her small pale fingers turn
bright red under the nails
then white
but after a few false starts
she snaps the blade halfway out,
pulling her fingers away quickly in surprise,
looks up at me with her deep blue eyes
glowing with pride

"Now the rest of the way."

less strain this time and the blade
snaps fully open

I hand her a stick and tell her to carve
always outward
away from herself
and soon the porch is littered with shavings
shining gold against the dark wood
in the late afternoon sun

as I watch she slowly carves
a rough wooden spoon
out of an old tree branch

it is too shallow to hold soup
and bristles with so many splinters
that I would be afraid to put it
anywhere near my mouth
but I pat her on the head and smile
and she smiles up at me
placing her spoon carefully on the step
amid the piles of shavings

"When you close it, hold your fingers out straight,
and push with your palm. Push once to close it halfway,
then again to close it all the way. And keep these
fingers back."

   it's getting late
   in the east the sky is already nearly black
   but in the west, in front of us
   the sun is just below the horizon,
   the clouds are streaked purple and gold

   she lays her head against my shoulder
   and puts her small hand in mine

"Dad?"

"Yuh?"

"Who taught you how to whittle?"

"My grandfather."

"He taught you lots of neat things, didn't he?"

"Yup."

"Will you teach them all to me?"

"I'll try."

Song in Two Movements

I

again the beach

sand machine-leveled
to the point where rough waters
have made a cliff
a two-foot drop

just below
a blue Man-o-War
puffed up

we keep our distance

wind off the ocean
warm   cooler back
under the evergreen trees
Australian pines
benches dotted beneath

sky wide with grey
clouds as far as the horizon

from the airport
just inland
the roar of jets
coming into sight
over the trees
disappearing into the grey
over the ocean

I cannot look at everything
hard enough

seagulls stand or strut
or fly above sand
course fragments of ageless
life come long ago
from the sea

tonight we will rise above
these trees   these birds
this beach
roaring over pines   over sand
and sea   into the grey night
into the frozen north

in our pockets   shells
    a few grains of sand

II

right now it is cold and no doubt
cloudy in Boston
students are returning to stand
in long lines in the bitter cold

the breeze on this beach
under these sighing trees
is cool under my light jacket
blows violently at the pages of my journal

it has been two weeks away
away from the same faces   same sounds
same people taken for granted
and taking
for granted

what is granted
is this life
this beach
with no prerequisites
  but time past

  shells ground to sand
  by the cold sea

no requirements
  but to look
    at everything
        hard

Southern Florida in Two Dimensions

On the highway you wait
to reach the top of a hill
for a longer view,
a further horizon.

But the horizon always
stays put, refusing
to retreat.

Even the sea
looks flat
from the narrow beaches.

Houses are one,
two stories at most.
A highrise apartment building
doesn't rise as high
as a small hotel in Boston.

But they have no more stars
at night than we up north,
though their sky seems able
to hold more clouds
than we ever see.

And when it rains
it seems the sun has gone
to look for a smaller home.

Serenade

the crescent of the moon
hangs downward
low
in the Florida sky
as if the tropical air
has made its burden of light
too heavy
to bear upright
as in the colder air
up north

we walk thru the cool evening
arms around each other
keeping warm
I hold my jacket closed at the neck

even so
the moon hangs down
weary from many tropical nights
past

an orange crescent sinking slowly
lengthwise into the waters
off Miami

Remembrance

As if
nothing
were happening
the hand sits,
then
the pen moves
across the page.

This seems
cadence enough.

But memory
once stirred
refuses to sleep
again.
Then it becomes
a struggle between
the will to continue
on, which is back
and the will to rest,
which is illusion.

Escape becomes
the only possibility,
whether through
or away.
Yet it is
escape
not from the self,
but into.

A cloud remembered,
and the touch of a hand,
warm, soft, young.

"It looks like a flying pig!"

And a laugh
beyond the grasp.

Chiseling a new self,
this night,
out of the coming day.
Grasping
the belief,
growing knowledge,
that pigs can
fly.

But all this
says nothing
of the billow of cloud,
like the head of a coldfront seen
in the museum, fifty thousand feet high,
chipped out of the evening sky,
towering down across the surface of the lake.

"I like the view from here;
this would be a nice house to live in,
you could see the whole lake."

"Yeah. Or that one over there..."

Unable to say, it was not that
house, or this view, but only
last night
I had walked this way alone,
had stopped to watch the sunset,
to look up at the open sky
reflected on the shallow pond,
and tonight,
I felt your hand
in mine.